MIKE BARTLETT

Mike Bartlett's plays include *Game* (Almeida); *King Charles III* (Almeida/West End/Broadway); *An Intervention* (Paines Plough/Watford Palace Theatre); *Bull* (Sheffield Theatres/ Off-Broadway); *Medea* (Glasgow Citizens/Headlong); *Chariots of Fire* (based on the film; Hampstead/West End); *13* (National Theatre); *Love, Love, Love* (Paines Plough/Plymouth Drum/ Royal Court); *Earthquakes in London* (Headlong/National Theatre); *Cock* (Royal Court/Off-Broadway); *Artefacts* (Nabokov/Bush); *Contractions* and *My Child* (Royal Court).

He was Writer-in-Residence at the National Theatre in 2011, and the Pearson Playwright-in-Residence at the Royal Court Theatre in 2007. *Cock* won an Olivier Award for Outstanding Achievement in an Affiliate Theatre in 2010. *Love, Love, Love* won the TMA Best New Play Award in 2011. *Bull* won the same award in 2013. *King Charles III* won the Critics' Circle Award for Best New Play in 2015.

Directing credits include *Medea* (Glasgow Citizens/Headlong); *Honest* (Northampton Royal & Derngate) and *Class* (Tristan Bates).

He has written seven plays for BBC Radio, winning the Writers' Guild Tinniswood and Imison prizes for *Not Talking*. His three-part television series, *The Town*, was broadcast on ITV1 in 2012 and nominated for a BAFTA for Breakthrough Talent, and his five-part series *Doctor Foster* premiered on BBC1 in 2015 and won Best New Drama at the National Television Awards.

He is currently developing television projects with the BBC, ITV, Big Talk, and Drama Republic, and under commission from Headlong Theatre, Liverpool Everyman and Playhouse, and the Royal Court Theatre.

Mike Bartlett

WILD

NICK HERN BOOKS

London

www.nickhernbooks.co.uk

A Nick Hern Book

Wild first published in Great Britain in 2016 as a paperback original by Nick Hern Books Limited, The Glasshouse, 49a Goldhawk Road, London W12 8QP

Wild copyright © 2016 Mike Bartlett

Mike Bartlett has asserted his right to be identified as the author of this work

Cover image by SWD; photography Shaun Webb

Designed and typeset by Nick Hern Books, London
Printed in Great Britain by CPI Group (UK) Ltd

A CIP catalogue record for this book is available from the British Library

ISBN 978 1 84842 572 9

Wild was first performed at Hampstead Theatre, London, on 11 June 2016, with the following cast:

WOMAN	Caoilfhionn Dunne
ANDREW	Jack Farthing
MAN	John Mackay

Director	James Macdonald
Designer	Miriam Buether
Lighting	Peter Mumford
Sound	Christopher Shutt

For Joseph

Characters

ANDREW
WOMAN
MAN

(/) *means the next speech begins at that point.*
(–) *means the next line interrupts.*
(…) *at the end of a speech means it trails off. On its own it indicates a pressure, expectation or desire to speak.*

A line with no full stop at the end indicates that the next speech follows on immediately.

A speech with no written dialogue indicates a character deliberately remaining silent.

This text went to press before the end of rehearsals and so may differ slightly from the play as performed.

1.

A nondescript hotel room.

ANDREW *is in the room.*

A WOMAN *has entered the room thirty seconds ago.*

ANDREW	Miss Prism?
WOMAN	That's right.
ANDREW	Is that a joke?
WOMAN	What?
ANDREW	Your name?
WOMAN	No.
ANDREW	Like a reference.
WOMAN	No.
ANDREW	A reference to –
WOMAN	It's not a reference.
	It's a coincidental pun.
	Which I thought you'd appreciate actually. And let me tell you, now you're in the club, that it's important to keep a sense of humour, because things are going to get, now and for the rest of your life, extremely difficult.
ANDREW	Well that's made me feel just rosy.
WOMAN	You want to know where it came from, the name?
ANDREW	Isn't it obvious?
WOMAN	No.
ANDREW	I'm fine.
	Beat.

WOMAN   You don't want to play. Okay. Do you want
           a drink?

ANDREW   No thank you.

WOMAN   I've got a sense, a feeling, I just know you want
           a gin and tonic? Something like that.

ANDREW   You're wrong.

           Beat.

WOMAN   I'd like one.

ANDREW   Okay.

           Beat.

WOMAN   I'm uneasy if it's just me. Not a party on my own,
           is it? If I have one will you have one?

ANDREW   I need to keep a clear head.

WOMAN   Why? Nothing's going to happen.

ANDREW   Well.

WOMAN   Nothing important's going to happen overnight,
           we're just going to talk and then tomorrow's
           another day.

ANDREW   Okay so we're going to talk, right, so I need to
           keep a clear head. Is he calling on the phone?

WOMAN   Who? Oh. You think he's going to call you on
           the phone?

ANDREW   They said he'd get in contact and he's hardly
           likely to turn up in person.

WOMAN   Why not?

ANDREW   He's trapped in an embassy in the middle of
           London.

WOMAN   Officially. Trapped is perhaps overstating it, the
           thing is we've got to make sure no one knows
           exactly where he is, so if he was coming to see
           you I wouldn't be able to tell you in advance, if
           you take my meaning.

ANDREW   So you're saying... what... he might come here?
           Tonight?

WOMAN   Look, you'll appreciate this when it's you – we
           couldn't have got you here without this kind of
           thing – the point is that *if* he's here, he's here, or if
           he's not here he's somewhere else. There are a lot
           of people who – let's not put too fine a point on it
           – want him dead, who are really out to kill him,
           and that's the club that you are part of now. You
           are Trotsky in Mexico, you are John Lennon in
           New York, Kennedy in fucking Texas.

ANDREW   Dallas.

WOMAN   I beg your pardon?

ANDREW   Kennedy got shot in Dallas.

WOMAN   Yeah, and Dallas is in Texas.

ANDREW   Yeah, I know, but...

WOMAN   Jesus this is your country.

ANDREW   I know – it doesn't matter.

WOMAN   We are very careful about saying where he is, and
           so long as you work with us, rest assured we're
           going to be equally careful about disclosing your
           location. I promise.

ANDREW   Good.

           Pause.

WOMAN   How are you doing?

ANDREW   Okay.

WOMAN   This is weird for you.

ANDREW   Yeah.

WOMAN   All this.

ANDREW   Weird yeah.

WOMAN   Like it happened just... overnight.

ANDREW   Well it did. Pretty much.

Beat.

WOMAN   You must have predicted it though, you must have known.

ANDREW   Yeah for a long time

But it's different, sat there at your desk, trying to work through all the consequences, just in your small life, trying to work out that the moment you click that button, you are going to have to walk out and your entire existence will change for ever, you know that's a difficult thing to imagine, I don't have that kind of imagination, I don't think anyone does. Last week, okay *last week,* last Thursday I wasn't in Russia, I wasn't being chased, I wasn't at risk of being assassinated, I was having chicken with my girlfriend in KFC, you understand what I'm talking about? –

WOMAN   Yeah.

ANDREW   – I was that guy, with his girl, we had plans, we were just doing our thing, our apartment, our post, our freaking parents and now... you know what I'm saying?

WOMAN   That's shocking.

ANDREW   Right.

WOMAN   You took your girlfriend to KFC?

ANDREW   You're really funny.

WOMAN   And she's still with you?

ANDREW   Well no she isn't. She's back home.

WOMAN   I mean she didn't break up with you? That's not what prompted all of this?

ANDREW   No.

WOMAN   So what the fuck were you doing in KFC?

ANDREW   That's not the point I was making.

WOMAN   I *know*. It's humour. See? I defused you. That's
         what I did, you were blowing up, I took a
         metaphorical pin, and I burst you. Like ppfff. And
         you just went ffffffffff.

ANDREW   You're a strange person.

WOMAN   Yes.

ANDREW   What's your – I don't even know who you are.

WOMAN   No.

ANDREW   What's your name?

WOMAN   I told you. Miss Prism.

ANDREW   Your real name not your James Bond name.

WOMAN   That is my real name.

ANDREW   No it isn't.

WOMAN   My full, real, name.

ANDREW   Your full name so your first name is Miss?

WOMAN   My first name is George.

ANDREW

WOMAN   George was the name of the first actor to play
         the part of Miss Prism in *The Importance of
         Being Earnest*.

ANDREW   I think you're gone completely crazy now.

WOMAN   A Trivial Comedy for Serious People. George was
         also a woman's name then, the part was played by
         a woman. I said actor because actress is politically
         incorrect. Anyway, I liked the name George Prism,
         so you can call me George, or Miss Prism,
         depending on your mood.

ANDREW   You liked the name George Prism.

WOMAN   Yes.

ANDREW   You chose it.

WOMAN   Had a certain charm.

ANDREW   So it's not your real name like you said it was.

          Beat.

WOMAN   I'm not very good at this.

ANDREW   You know I betrayed my entire country in an act
          that means I could be electrocuted and killed by
          my own politicians, I then flew to Hong Kong
          where I recorded an interview which was broadcast
          around the world, spent two days hiding in a pod-
          style hotel in Moscow Airport, before being
          smuggled onto a plane as luggage then back off the
          plane, and eventually across the Russian border,
          but despite all that circus or strangeness, I'd say
          this, you, this moment now, is head and shoulders
          the weirdest part of it. You are a fucking nutfuck.

          Pause.

          Isn't there anyone else to talk to?

WOMAN   You speak Russian?

ANDREW   No.

WOMAN   You should learn.

ANDREW   Let's wait and see if I need to.

WOMAN   Well while you're waiting… I'm the only person
          to talk to.

ANDREW   Shit.

WOMAN   Yeah.

          Beat.

          Nightmare stuck in the room with the nutjob
          nutfuck. You sure you don't want a drink? Do
          you miss her?

ANDREW   What?

WOMAN   Your girlfriend. What's her name again?

ANDREW   I didn't tell you.

WOMAN   Oh. Yes. Sorry. What's her name?

ANDREW   Cindy.

WOMAN   No come on her real name.

ANDREW   What?

WOMAN   Oh, you mean… you mean it really is? Wow.

ANDREW   What?

WOMAN   Well. You're, like, American? And your girlfriend is like, called Cindy? Isn't that, like, oh my god? Like… weirdass?

ANDREW   Why?

WOMAN   Cindy. You know, like the doll.

ANDREW   It's not like the doll. The doll is Sindy with an 'S'.

WOMAN   Makes no difference

ANDREW   And also Sindy was British, not American. America had Barbie.

WOMAN   How do you know this? How long have you known her?

           Cindy.

           Beat.

ANDREW   Since I was seventeen.

WOMAN   High school.

ANDREW   Right.

WOMAN   High-school sweethearts.

ANDREW   Well.

WOMAN   That's so *cool* dude, that's like, so rad.

ANDREW   Enjoying yourself?

WOMAN   Do you miss her?

ANDREW   Of course I miss her. I miss everybody… and I don't know. I don't even know what's happened to them, if they've been called in for questioning –

WOMAN   They have.

ANDREW   And I don't know by who…

WOMAN   The CIA.

ANDREW   And where they are and what they're being asked…

WOMAN   They're being asked if they had any notion of what you planned to do, whether they had anything to do with it, whether they currently have any contact with you, whether they have plans to join you, and if they have any sense of what your future movements might be, I would imagine that assuming neither your girlfriend, your friends or your parents say anything even slightly incriminating they'll be let free from questioning in two maybe three weeks.

ANDREW   Okay.

    Beat.

WOMAN   I mean what you did is big.

ANDREW   I know.

WOMAN   Off-the-scale massive.

ANDREW   Yeah.

WOMAN   And the thing is that as we now know they can get access to all your emails web-browsing phone lines, and it's been a few days so any encryption you used, I'd imagine they're through that, so they don't really need to ask those people anything, if they go through the files they probably have it already.

ANDREW   Yeah.

WOMAN   So why are they bringing them in like that?

ANDREW   To put pressure on me.

WOMAN   Correct, they're actually hoping that you do still have some kind of contact with Mindy –

ANDREW   Cindy

WOMAN   – or your parents and that by bringing them in and cutting them off and making their lives hell, you

will break and snap and get on a plane and give
yourself up, driven by the innate national pride
that's been bred in you from the moment you were
born in the USA. This is why all the kids in your
weirdass motherfucking country swear allegiance
to the flag and all that shit. Precisely to ensure that
you don't do things like this.

ANDREW   They won't hurt them.

WOMAN   You don't think?

ANDREW   Will they?

WOMAN   I don't –

ANDREW   I'm asking you.

WOMAN   Oh. I don't know. No. Can they? No. Surely
that's illegal.

ANDREW   But – there might be psychological –

WOMAN   Oh sorry well yeah psychological stuff absolutely,
isolation, intimidation, lies, deceit and a slow
breaking-down of self-esteem they'll try all that,
they'll do that to them but that's okay because
none of that stuff is real or hurts or has any long-
lasting effect, oh wait – it does.

ANDREW   You find this funny?

WOMAN   You know I actually don't find any of this funny at
all no.

Pause.

ANDREW   Okay.

Pause.

WOMAN   You want to pick up that phone and call Sandy?

ANDREW   That's not her name.

WOMAN   You'd like Susie to hear your voice?

ANDREW   We were together twelve years of course I want to
pick up the phone and speak to her.

WOMAN   But you understand you really shouldn't?

ANDREW   Yeah.

WOMAN   Try it.

ANDREW   What?

WOMAN   Try and pick up that phone and call Lindsey.

ANDREW   *Cindy.*

WOMAN   Go on.

ANDREW   I don't want to.

WOMAN   I know but try it.

ANDREW   You're getting really fucking irritating.

WOMAN   Yeah I know so go on just go over there and try
          and call her.

          He does.

          You see?

ANDREW   No dialling tone.

WOMAN   You know why?

ANDREW   What?

WOMAN   We had it disconnected before you got here.

ANDREW   Okay.

WOMAN   You know why?

ANDREW   …

WOMAN   We don't trust you. For all we know this could be
          some kind of infiltration, you could be someone
          actually working for the FBI, the CIA, the British
          Secret Service, the British Metropolitan Police, they
          all conduct secret operations lasting years we know
          this now, and there's no real limits in practice on
          what they can do, on the situations they can get
          themselves in so we now have everyone under
          suspicion the whole time because in the end we

can't know. None of us can know. The only way we
develop trust in the end is… well… time.

ANDREW   …

WOMAN   Time.

ANDREW   …

WOMAN   Because you only have one life. And every week,
every month you're stuck in undercover work,
you're using it up, and most people aren't
prepared to do more than a few months of that, so
by the time you've been with the movement for
years, like me, people pretty much know that I am
who I say I am.

ANDREW   George.

WOMAN   Exactly.

ANDREW   Which is not your real name.

WOMAN   You've been with us three days Andrew, of course
it's not my real fucking name.

Pause.

ANDREW   I'm not with you.

WOMAN   Yes.

ANDREW   I'm not.

WOMAN   According to the entire world's press you are, you
might be having this meeting, where you're staying,
this has all been arranged by us, you're with us.

ANDREW   I've said nothing about what you do, I've made no
commitments.

WOMAN   You've been willing to take advantage of our
expertise.

ANDREW   You said you valued what I'd done and you
offered your help.

WOMAN   And you quickly took it.

ANDREW   I know I'm associated but I don't think I'm *part* of anything right now. Right now I'm pretty much on my own –

WOMAN   Well. Yeah. You are. No one else has ever done what you've done.

ANDREW   No.

WOMAN   In the history of the world, it's simply not been possible, to release as much as you have so quickly. With such effect. You have leaked such a huge amount of metaphorical fluid, it's like a tsunami of liquid just sprayed over them, covering them –

Isn't it?

And it's not just scale, it's how important this stuff is, its depth, its height. It's like you've blown the biggest fucking whistle you can imagine, like a whistle the size of the Pentagon. You've blown that massive Pentagonal whistle really fucking hard.

I don't think the USA has a punishment proportional to people like you.

Do they?

I mean they can only kill you once.

ANDREW   Maybe leave me on my own now?

WOMAN   Come on. No. What? Really?

ANDREW   Really.

WOMAN   You like me being here.

ANDREW   Haven't you got anything else to do?

WOMAN   No.

ANDREW   You must.

WOMAN   Do you fancy me?

ANDREW   Jesus.

WOMAN   come on

ANDREW   No.

WOMAN   You do.

ANDREW   No.

WOMAN   I've been getting a vibe, if I can call it that –

ANDREW   No you haven't.

WOMAN   Do I look like Cindy?

ANDREW   No.

WOMAN   How am I different?

ANDREW   Cindy's blonde.

WOMAN   I'm blonde.

ANDREW   No you're not.

WOMAN   Underneath.

ANDREW   Okay.

WOMAN   This is dyed.

ANDREW   No it isn't.

WOMAN   Okay it isn't. I'm attractive though, an objectively
attractive person, It's not a matter of opinion.

ANDREW   No.

WOMAN   Yeah.

ANDREW   No.

WOMAN   A bit.

ANDREW   Stop. Just stop. Stop.

Beat.

WOMAN   How else?

ANDREW   What?

WOMAN   How else am I different to Cindy Windy Cindy?

ANDREW   Cindy's funny.

WOMAN   Ah. Clever.

ANDREW   Yes she is. Exactly.

WOMAN   I mean you were clever with your little insult there. But okay Cindy's clever what has she got then?

ANDREW   She's –

WOMAN   Qualifications. Did she go to Cambridge?

ANDREW   Of course not.

WOMAN   I did.

ANDREW   Well done.

WOMAN   Thanks it was really hard.

ANDREW   Who are you?

WOMAN   University though okay you're saying she went to university.

ANDREW   No after high school she went straight into business.

WOMAN   Okay, so when you say clever we're talking street smarts here, we're not talking actual proper university, knowing things, useful proper intelligence.

ANDREW   Fuck you.

WOMAN   She's not part of the intellectual elite, like me.

ANDREW   Jesus –

WOMAN   I can quote Latin.

ANDREW   I honestly don't care what you / can do, so maybe just stop talking until you can say something that is genuinely and actually going to offer me something or help me out cos what I don't need at the moment is more… noise. Okay. You're still… okay…

WOMAN   You think that's not useful it actually is. Dinner parties in high-level company pretty girl quoting Latin they are eating out of my hand, I'm telling you they should teach that at school, bring it back, they used to teach both those things being pretty and speaking Latin I can see why. Okay. Okay so you don't fancy me. We'll leave that for now, but so

that you know I don't fancy you at all, not in a sex
way, but I think we're getting on we are, we are.
You and me, this is a thing, this is a relationship
you're going to remember.

ANDREW   That's true.

WOMAN   Ita vero.

That's Latin for 'yeah'.

Beat.

ANDREW   Why are you here?

WOMAN   Well far be it for me to remind you Andrew but
you released hundred of thousands of highly
confidential –

ANDREW   I mean here in this room now, you could be doing
some other work, there's a security guard outside
to protect me, presumably when he gets here he
gets here –

WOMAN   – *if* he gets here –

ANDREW   – and there's nothing I or you can do to hurry that
up so why are you keeping me company like this?

WOMAN   You want the truth or something that will make
you feel good?

ANDREW   The truth won't make me feel good?

WOMAN   The truth will not.

ANDREW   Okay.

WOMAN   The truth will make you feel even shitter than you
do right now.

And I can see how inside, you're upset, and crying
and nearly panicking, you're covering it well, it's
not as bad as I would have imagined, but you
might not want me to lay on even more right at
this moment.

ANDREW   Just tell me why – yes – tell me the truth. Why are
you here?

WOMAN   You know why, I'm liaising with him about –

ANDREW   I mean right now, you've got nothing to add, or
          offer, we're waiting for him to make contact so
          why are you still in the room? Saying all this crap,
          goofing around?

          Beat.

WOMAN   We're worried you might kill yourself.

ANDREW   I...

          Really?

WOMAN   Hmm. Yeah.

          Beat.

          I mean this is a thing that we've been noticing
          and it makes complete sense, the media and
          governments and corporations are yet to admit it,
          but these days when someone like you, a
          whistleblower, or it could equally be someone
          that's really fucked up in their job and got the
          blame, or it could be someone accused falsely or
          not of a crime, or even the victim of a crime, but
          any of these people, when the full spotlight of the
          media the information, the internet is on them with
          millions, really millions of people talking about
          them – this is a truly contemporary phenomenon –
          these people, like you, have the certain knowledge
          that this moment will define them in the eyes of
          everyone they meet from now on for the rest of
          their lives, that it is now actually impossible for
          this not to be what their entire life is all about.
          We've noticed, and we're not pretending that this
          needs science or anything, we've noticed that at
          about the stage of the story you're at now, they
          often try to take their own life and sometimes they
          succeed, we're talking Dr David Kelly, he's
          probably the best example, but there was also that
          woman in hospital, the nurse who answered the
          phone to the Australian hoax DJs, who wanted the

medical information about Kate and William, you remember, you remember that?

ANDREW   No.

WOMAN   Oh. Maybe it was just a British… Anyway, point is, millions of people hate you now, and short of drastic facial surgery and some kind of new identity this is what your life is going to be about. You're twenty-eight and you will never be known for research, or politics, or art, or music, or sport, or charity, or anything else, you will be for ever known solely for what you did three days ago.

ANDREW   You're working me up to it.

WOMAN   I'm naming it to make it less likely.

Beat.

ANDREW   How would I kill myself in this room?

WOMAN   We took away anything obvious but there's still… well I'm not going to lay them out for you, am I! Huh! Clever… but yeah there's actually still a few ways, looking at it, that I could think of –

ANDREW   I'm fine. I'm not going to do anything.

WOMAN   That's strange. Yes. I can see that, you appear quite calm.

But that's odd. Most people would *freak OUT* right now, but you're not. Why not?

ANDREW   I told you I worked it through, obviously not all the details, and yeah, I suppose, I am freaking out to some extent.

WOMAN   To some extent. Yeah. A bit. Not a lot though. Not a reasonable *human* amount.

ANDREW   It wouldn't do any good.

WOMAN   Pragmatism.

ANDREW   I suppose.

Beat.

WOMAN   Were you running away from something?

ANDREW   No.

WOMAN   Was there a push for you as well as a pull?

ANDREW   No, it was – what I saw, I just couldn't in all conscience –

WOMAN   Yeah I've seen in the interview I didn't entirely buy it then either. I mean there's loads of people like you working there and in all sorts of jobs who think this stuff but none of them are prepared to jack in their *entire life*. There must be a reason this appealed, you can't be that selfless.

ANDREW   Well... I don't know what to say. Except your lack of belief in people is really upsetting.

WOMAN   *No*. No. I think people can be good, just not on the scale that you're talking about with these sort of consequences. Either you didn't realise the consequences –

ANDREW   I did.

WOMAN   Yeah I think you did. Or you did, but you thought it was worth it because you're so fucking altruistic.

ANDREW   Right.

WOMAN   Hmm. OR – there's a third option which is that the life you're now embarking on is, in your judgement, preferable to the one you left behind, and yes – that's what I think is going on.

ANDREW   What, like I killed someone, or –

WOMAN   No.

ANDREW   You know committed a crime and now I'm running away.

WOMAN   No I don't think it needs to be anything like that. I just think you might have been incredibly bored.

              I think maybe you craved some kind of true adventure.

ANDREW   That's trivialising it – you know I am at risk of
           death either by an assassin or my own country –

WOMAN   My grandmother was Jewish, lived in Poland, she
           had to escape from the Nazis across Europe, her
           family died, and then when she got to Britain she
           had to learn another culture and language, and still
           she was being bombed, and attacked, and then
           bring her family up with a second husband, then
           emigrate to Australia, a country she knew even
           less about, then come back, and in the meantime
           she published twenty-three books and met an
           unfeasible number of famous and important
           people. I mean lives like that don't happen any
           more not in that kind of continent-crossing, life-
           and-death, history-making, autobiography-busting
           way. I'm not saying they wanted it but that
           generation's lives were eventful. To say the least.

ANDREW   Right.

WOMAN   Compare that to you, and Cindy, in Kentucky
           Fricking Chicken –

ANDREW   Look –

WOMAN   I'm not being facetious it's a fact that with the
           homogenisation of branding, with the transfer of
           information from continent to continent the
           possibility for mystery and real travel and
           adventure has actually lessened. All countries have
           a McDonald's, the vast majority of places can be
           looked up on Google Maps, what are the chances of
           truly exploring? A man finds a twelve-metre
           waterfall in Canada that no one's bothered to write
           down, it makes headline news these days around
           the world? So what are the chances of truly
           exploring, truly changing. Zero. Unless. Andrew.
           You're you. You changed the world three days ago.

ANDREW   You think that.

WOMAN   I do.

           Actually?

I think you may have brought down the United
States of America.

ANDREW   Right.

WOMAN   Not overnight. But China is laughing at them.
The last remaining high ground they occupied,
that of freedom, has been taken from them. Turns
out, from what you've shown us, they spy on their
people exactly the same way the party does in
Shanghai, exactly the same way the KGB or
whatever you want to call it does in Russia – you,
Andrew, have proven this as a fact. The USA is
not free, and it's worse than anywhere else,
because unlike China, or Russia, that was the
whole point of that country. That was its USP.
Its raison d'être. The primary principle upon
which the fathers did the founding. To be free,
from the governments, the masters, the rules of
oppressive regimes and churches. That was the
high ground it should have occupied, and so far
has your country fallen Andrew. So far now.

ANDREW   I don't want to destroy it. I want to restore the
balance between the elected and the electorate.
I want the country to get better.

WOMAN   It can't. It either is the thing it is, or it doesn't
exist. America has always used all the powers
possible. It's a torturing country, it's a spying
country, it's a country that props up dictators, and
funds terrorism. It does all the things it says it
fights against, in service to some greater cause
which it calls freedom. But if now, you say it
never even had that... well...

It's the latest icon to fall.
We find that nothing is noble.
Nothing is righteous.
Nothing is good.

ANDREW   Whether you want to believe it or not I actually
love my country, I did what I did in the hope that
it will get better, that it will prompt action.

WOMAN   It won't.

ANDREW   You don't know.

WOMAN   It will prompt proposals to action and the specific
practices you uncovered will cease, for a while.
But others will continue. The issue is that it's either
a technological problem or a governmental one.

ANDREW   Can we talk about something else?

WOMAN   Either you say the government is good but
technology has got too powerful and has to be
reined in somehow, or, you say technology is good
but the power of government has to be reined in.
No one can agree, so nothing happens.

ANDREW   What about corporations?

WOMAN   Well that's a whole other thing.

ANDREW   Do you have a boyfriend?

WOMAN   Ah – well – oh – Not a boyfriend no.

ANDREW   Girlfriend then?

WOMAN   I have a relationship with a horse.

ANDREW   OH!

WOMAN   What?

ANDREW   Okay – just – don't –

WOMAN   He fucks me like – wooah – Jesus you wouldn't
imagine, he goes out racing, I watch, then we go
for dinner, you know somewhere classy like
Burger King, then back to his, we lie on the straw,
and... well it's not to everyone's taste but – talk
about reining it in.

ANDREW   You couldn't have just said I can't tell you?

WOMAN   No because I can tell you, it's not the army, we're
all, I can tell you what I want, I choose not to
because I don't *know* you.

ANDREW   Right.

WOMAN   So much like the government of your country,
           I prefer to remain in the shadows and distract
           you with whimsy.

ANDREW   Isn't that quite a contradiction for an organisation
           that advocates full disclosure?

WOMAN   Yeah well absolutely and that's not the half of it,
           we've got quite a lot of contradiction going on, as
           you'll find out. I mean don't for god's sake look
           for a coherent set of values or a constructive way
           forward in us lot. I mean we're not that far off a
           bunch of fucking anarchists, it's like herding cats,
           like taming fucking I don't know… plants. As far
           as I can work out, and there's nothing really
           written down about this – which is a very
           contemporary way for a protest group to operate –
           in cells you know – the very definition of 'wiki' –
           so as far as I can work out, the only principle on
           which we operate is that governments cannot
           proclaim to be working for the people if they
           withhold huge amounts of information from the
           people. How can they be accountable if the
           majority of what they do that's important is
           restricted? How do we know what really happened
           in Afghanistan or Iraq, or with the police, or
           Hillsborough or Stephen Lawrence, or phone
           hacking? Are these references too British for you?

ANDREW   Some of them.

WOMAN   Then Watergate, Union Carbide, Bush's win in
           Florida, I mean we really want to allow these
           people to hide behind confidentiality laws?
           Which would mean that at the ballot box we're
           just guessing? But yeah, when it comes to the
           actual people that do it – me or him, to take two
           examples, we're both incredibly secretive.
           I suppose the difference is we don't profess
           anything else. We're not saying trust us. We're
           saying just look at the information.

ANDREW   Okay.

WOMAN   You interested in any of this?

ANDREW   Well you know I kind of think I'm done now, I'm
            not going to make a habit of it so –

WOMAN   Well you can't mate.

ANDREW   No.

WOMAN   You've shot your load.

ANDREW   Yeah.

WOMAN   So what now? That's the question. That's what's
            of interest to us. What happens to you now?

ANDREW   Do you have friends?

WOMAN   Yes. Loads. Uni friends mostly. We're a tight-knit
            group. Argue into the night issues of politics,
            society, high-level intelligent debate about actually
            no I don't have any friends I work too hard.

            You see? You just can't tell.

            Pause.

ANDREW   I will have that drink.

WOMAN   I thought you might.

ANDREW

WOMAN

ANDREW   …

WOMAN   Lonely.

ANDREW   Right at this moment, I am. Yes.

WOMAN   You don't give a shit about any of all of that now
            do you? You just want a hug.

ANDREW   …

            She edges closer.

            Then squeezes his shoulder, awkwardly.

WOMAN   Is that okay? Thought a hug might be a bit…
         much?

         So… just thought I'd give you a… *squeeze*?

         She does it again.

         Then pats him.

         It'll be okay.

         Her hand comes to rest on him.

         Your parents are called Ellen and Harry.

ANDREW   Yes they are.

WOMAN   You see I know that.

ANDREW   Yes I can see that you know that well.

WOMAN   You know what else I know?

ANDREW   What?

WOMAN   Your SAT scores for every year you took them.

ANDREW   Okay.

WOMAN   You know what else?

ANDREW   What?

WOMAN   Pretty much everything I know about Sam, I know
         about Michael, I know about Terri – oh – oh well
         I know about Sara. I know the car you drive, sorry,
         drove, I know the clothes you wore when you were
         seventeen with the… wow – *hair*, I know where
         you've been on holiday every time you've been to
         another country which isn't that many, if we don't
         count Hawaii which we shouldn't, in fact you've
         doubled that number in the last couple of days.

ANDREW   Of course you know all that, it's on Facebook,
         Instagram, a child could probably find out all of
         that –

WOMAN   Yeah, that's my point, the fact is that if anyone
         really wants to know about someone else now,

you can. That's just how it is, you have no privacy really you have no rights –

ANDREW   You do have rights –

WOMAN   Oh okay you do, but, you know, in reality, as soon as you get a Google account or go on Facebook whatever and you tick that little box with all the terms and conditions that you never read, you don't. And it goes further than that if we were going to expend all this energy helping you out we had to go as deep as possible, so I'm not just talking stuff you can find on Facebook, I'm talking *everything*, I think probably I know more about you than anyone else on the planet right now, I certainly know more than your parents or Cindy, I think I possibly know more than you do about yourself given the amount of cannabis you smoked at college. So you want to know anything about yourself just ask.

ANDREW   I don't.

WOMAN   Test me.

ANDREW   I really don't. You know why? Because none of that makes any difference now. This is like the blankest cleanest slate I could start with. I have a single bag of stuff and that's it, that's all I now own. I know you, here, and that's it. As you've pointed out I don't speak Russian, I'm not sure how I'm going to survive here. I don't know how to get food, I can't read this fucking alphabet. It's *all* strange to me here, all alien, I don't know what's going to happen tomorrow, or next month or next year, where I'm going to move on to, or what my life is about. I don't know what my future is – if Cindy going's to come out and stay or –

WOMAN   I thought you split up with Cindy.

ANDREW   You said you knew everything about me.

WOMAN   I do. I thought you split up with Cindy.

ANDREW   –

WOMAN   –

ANDREW   That was the last call I made.

WOMAN   Right.

ANDREW   To break up with her.

WOMAN   You knew what was going to happen and you made her believe you didn't love her any more.

ANDREW   Yeah.

WOMAN   Problem is, when she found out what you did, she worked out why you broke up with her, and she doesn't believe it and she's still in love with you and determined to find you, so that plan didn't work, you should be lucky we're handling that side of things now, because from the evidence you are a bit shit at it.

ANDREW   Is he coming then?

Beat.

Or is he going to call me?

Beat.

Or not?

Pause.

WOMAN   You want to know some things about Russia?

Beat.

You want to know some things about Russia?

ANDREW   I can look on Wikipedia.

WOMAN   I'm more fun. Your laptop's gone mysteriously missing anyway. And you don't have a phone so –

ANDREW   No I do. I don't have a charger that fits to sockets on the wall so it's not working right now but I do have one. It's in my case.

WOMAN   It's not. We took it.

ANDREW   Give it back.

WOMAN   For your own good. As you are aware, if you have a phone, they can find out where you are.

Pause.

So you want to know some things then?

ANDREW   About Russia.

WOMAN   Yeah.

ANDREW   What?

WOMAN   Population?

ANDREW   ?

WOMAN   144 million.

ANDREW   Okay.

WOMAN   It's bigger than Pluto.

ANDREW   Right.

WOMAN   Each Russian, on average, consumes eighteen litres of alcohol per year, double what experts consider dangerous.

ANDREW   What do you want me to do with that?

WOMAN   This is where you are and I think it's important you know the facts.

ANDREW   Why?

WOMAN   Because I don't think you're that bright, Andrew. I think you're actually a little bit stupid – I'm not being mean here, but if you're going to survive, if you're going to make any contribution going forward the only thing you can rely on is your brain and your ability to articulate yourself. You're fucking Nick Leeson, by which I don't mean you're fucking Nick Leeson, I mean that's the equivalent of who you are. He could only make a meaningful contribution and do so well in the 'media' after he got out of jail because he had a unique combination of experience and intelligence. Now you have a unique experience but your intelligence needs work.

ANDREW   I'm smart.

WOMAN   You don't know who Nick Leeson is, do you?

ANDREW   Another British reference?

WOMAN   Er – yeah, but that doesn't mean you shouldn't know it. I know loads of Americans and I'm British – well – sort of –

ANDREW   I was employed by the US Government at an extremely high level, which should give some indication of –

WOMAN   You're medium smart, you're red-brick, middle-scale, mid-league bright, but you need to be elite Oxford Harvard bright.

ANDREW   I went to Harvard.

WOMAN   Why are you lying? I know where you went.

ANDREW   I was testing you because I wanted to do something in the conversation.

WOMAN   Then say something – have something to offer and say something.

ANDREW   …

WOMAN   This is what I mean you don't have it click click like off the tip of your tongue, it takes a thought, but you need it right there.

ANDREW   Why?

WOMAN   If you're going to become a spokesperson for us.

ANDREW   Spokesperson?

WOMAN   That's the current idea.

ANDREW   No.

WOMAN   Well we're going to want *something* back for all this –

ANDREW   I'm not going to become a spokesperson for you.

WOMAN   You're very respected at the moment and the feeling is you'd restore some creditability to our once-esteemed organisation. We've got a bit stuck in scandal recently –

ANDREW   I'm not becoming a face for your organisation so –

WOMAN   Andrew you have absolutely no choice.

ANDREW   I do.

WOMAN   No. You have no freedom, no choice, at the moment you don't even have a passport. You are in this country but you have no rights and currently no asylum. To get any or all of these things you are going to need help and contacts. We have them, but we aren't going to give them to you for free. We want you to be our man in Moscow.

ANDREW   Where?

WOMAN   *Moscow*. That's where you currently are.

ANDREW   I know I meant what does that mean? 'Your man in – '

WOMAN   It's a Graham Greene reference. You see? You don't know shit. You don't even know where you are. This isn't a charitable thing. This transaction. This is a deal.

ANDREW   But I don't subscribe to your policy.

WOMAN   We don't really have one as I said before. We all have disagreements all the time.

ANDREW   But there are big disagreements I have.

WOMAN   Fine. The only thing you need to be committed to is freedom of information. And even that you can be nuanced on. At the moment you've got one of the most retweeted, pictured and repictured faces on the planet. That's good. That's what's got you this room, this hotel, that's what we're funding. Come on you know that.

ANDREW   So I have to –

WOMAN   You have to check with us what you want to say
          about stuff and assuming it's not completely off
          beam and weird then go for it. When things happen.

ANDREW   From Russia.

WOMAN   Moscow yes. This is where you'll live.

          Pause.

          So. What? Why aren't you talking now? What's
          going on?

ANDREW   I'm not going to stay in Moscow for ever –

WOMAN   Why not?

ANDREW   I don't need to join you.

WOMAN   We're going to help you.

ANDREW   You're going to help me yes, because it benefits
          you. You need me.

WOMAN   Don't step to me small man.

ANDREW   – like you said this is probably the most important
          leak ever – in terms of impact this dwarfs what
          you've done before – and more than that, it justifies
          itself in clearer ways. You want me associated with
          you, because you need me, because, I'm right, in
          this instance – people are realising that I'm
          incontrovertibly justified, which was not the same
          with all the military secrets you put out.

WOMAN   Not me.

ANDREW   Your organisation.

WOMAN   Well we're getting into collective responsibility
          now.

ANDREW   Okay let's get into that then.

WOMAN   We don't really – that's not how we work, we're
          more like an idea that is constantly evolving
          depending on the views of the current members
          and the response to the need of the – oh okay I'm
          not even convincing myself. Yes we make, made,

mistakes, not ones I'm particularly into justifying
I didn't want to release all of that I said it would
do us harm and it did.

ANDREW   He ordered it didn't he?

WOMAN   He... did. Yes he did.

ANDREW   Despite all of you saying it was a bad idea.

WOMAN   That's correct.

ANDREW   So why do you still work for him?

WOMAN   Because ultimately he's vain, and he's doing this
more for himself than for anybody else, and he has
a very dark side which we won't go into, but
ultimately underneath all that (and maybe you
need all that to do what he does) but underneath
all that, the basic idea of what he's doing is right.

ANDREW   You could be talking about Stalin.

WOMAN   Oh. Please. No. Don't do that. The basic idea is
right, but the nature of it being so loosely
controlled is that it's loosely controlled – however
I suppose the appeal for me – and maybe this is
not so different from what you described earlier
Andrew – is that I may be a player, or at the very
least present when events happen which change
the course of history. I may be part of that and if
I am close to those events I may be able to alter
them. And to my extremely clever mind, that is
a good use of my resources, even if it means
hanging out with people I don't like very much,
and being close to decisions I don't agree with.

ANDREW   The fact is, you need me more than I need you.

Pause.

WOMAN   You think that?

ANDREW   All this time you're speaking with me. The money
you must have spent for the accommodation and
lawyers.

As you said yourself, I represent a chance for you to get back in the game. To restore your credibility.

Beat.

No.

WOMAN   I thought we were getting on...

ANDREW   I am not being your spokesperson. If you're offering help that's great, and I've no doubt you'll tell everyone you're helping me, but you don't get anything actively in return from me, I'm not going to be part of your group, or any group. I'm not going to become a face for hire. I'm just... me.

WOMAN   I see.

Well... In that case I'll tell him you're not interested.

ANDREW   Sure.

WOMAN   He won't make contact.

ANDREW   Okay.

WOMAN   We'll leave you in the hotel tonight, then you're on your own. It's a shame but –

ANDREW   You're going to help me anyway, what I represent –

WOMAN   How's the Russian?

ANDREW   I can wait.

WOMAN   Not great is it, but anyway dossvidanija, I hope you get to see the dostoprimechatelnosti before you get kicked out.

ANDREW   You need to be associated with me.

WOMAN   Are you going to help us out?

Andrew?

Last chance?

Wanna play ball?

No?

Okay.

Have a think.

See you later.

Maybe.

She smiles and goes.

He stands for a moment.

Then blackout.

2.

A while later.

A knock at the door.

ANDREW	Who is it?

A MAN *enters, wearing a suit. He's very serious.*

MAN	Hi.
ANDREW	Is it open?
MAN	Yes.
	Andrew.
ANDREW	Are you.
MAN	What?
ANDREW	Are you him? You don't –
MAN	Who?
ANDREW	Him?
MAN	Er… I don't know if you should be expecting me. Did you know I was coming?
ANDREW	That depends who you are.
MAN	My name is George.
ANDREW	George?
MAN	I'm here to help you. He sent me.
ANDREW	He…
MAN	Yes, you know –
ANDREW	I'm… I've been told I should stay here and that he'll make contact –
MAN	Er – don't think so. Ha! Who told you that?

ANDREW   The other, the…

MAN   What? Other?

ANDREW   The lady. It doesn't matter.

MAN   Lady?

ANDREW   There was a lady?

MAN   What lady?

ANDREW   Sent by him, working with him, she was looking after me while I waited to see him. She worked for him.

MAN   I work for him.

ANDREW   You… what?

MAN   There isn't a lady. Hasn't been a lady. He sent me here to help you out. He's trapped, you know he can't leave London, that's why he sent me.

ANDREW   Wait – there was a woman. A lady who said she was…

MAN   Was?

ANDREW   …okay…

MAN   What did you tell her?

ANDREW   I don't – a lot.

MAN   Where's she gone?

ANDREW   She left.

MAN   When?

ANDREW   A hour ago. Not long.

MAN   She's not working for us.

ANDREW   How do you know?

MAN   Are you listening, Andrew, I know because I work for him and she doesn't. What did you tell her?

ANDREW   …nothing.

MAN   Really?

ANDREW   She seemed to know most things already.

MAN   She... right. Excellent. Right. Well...

             That's a shame.

ANDREW   So you're...

MAN   George.

             Hello.

             What was her name?

ANDREW   ...she called herself Miss Prism.

MAN   First name?

ANDREW   Of course I knew it wasn't her real name.

MAN   Did she give a first name?

ANDREW   George.

MAN   What?

ANDREW   George.

MAN   Yes?

ANDREW   *She said her first name was George.*

MAN   George is a boy's name.

ANDREW   Well that's what I said.

MAN   George is *my* name.

             Beat.

             I think she was playing with you.

ANDREW   So who was she?

MAN   Did you ask her for any identification?

ANDREW   No but... presumably even if I did she could have
             got it forged.

MAN   That's true.

ANDREW   So she could have been anything? Anyone.

Journalist. Spy.

MAN   Right.

ANDREW   And I told her...

MAN   What?

ANDREW   Well actually she seemed to know a lot about me already.

MAN   Everyone knows everything about you Andrew. It's everywhere. You can't very well do what you did and then ask for any kind of privacy. You are probably the most open target in terms of digging for dirt, you better not have done anything too weird. Ever.

ANDREW   I haven't.

MAN   Ever.

ANDREW   I really haven't.

MAN   You – Oh come on Andrew. Everyone's done something weird at some point.

Haven't they?

I have.

Haven't they?

ANDREW

Pause.

So she knows where I am.

MAN   Yes apparently she does.

The MAN *reaches into his case.*

Chocolate. Thought you might want it. Sugar levels.

ANDREW   Yeah.

ANDREW *takes it, and eats it.*

MAN   So. I need to assess you for help.

ANDREW   Have you got any identification?

MAN   What?

ANDREW   You're saying she could have been anyone and
           I should have asked for identification so have you?

           The MAN *reaches into his pocket and gives*
           ANDREW *his passport.*

           This is your passport.

MAN   Right.

ANDREW   Well no, that just tells me who you are –

MAN   That's what identification means Andrew.

ANDREW   I need to know who you work for. If you're really
           acting for him.

MAN   What you mean... like... a membership card?

ANDREW   No.

MAN   We're not a *gym.*

ANDREW   I don't know – papers.

MAN   *Papers?*

ANDREW   Something.

MAN   Well I suppose the passport is who I am, and you
           could google me or something and that would tell
           you – or call someone.

ANDREW   I can't call someone.

MAN   Why not?

ANDREW   They disconnected the phone. They – the woman
           – the phone was disconnected.

MAN   No it isn't.

ANDREW   What?

MAN   The phone's working. Call someone if you like
           and check me out.

           ANDREW *stands and goes to the phone. Picks
           it up.*

           See?

           Puts it down again.

ANDREW   I can't think of anyone I could call that you
           couldn't have influenced. I don' t think there's
           really any way of me knowing who you are. For
           sure. Any more than with her.

MAN   Andrew –

ANDREW   Is there?

MAN   Maybe not. And that's because you don't have
           a team. You don't have resources. You have your
           journalist friends, and they help you get information
           but they can't look after you not in the end. They
           can't look at someone and say yes, that is who they
           say they are. We can do that for you. I can do that.
           I'm not him but I'm his right-hand man with the
           same resources at my disposal. I can protect you.

ANDREW   But only if you are really working for who you
           say you are.

MAN   Yes.

ANDREW   So how do I know?

MAN   It looks like you've reached the point where
           you're going to have to trust someone.

           Beat.

           You don't have long, Andrew. You realise that?
           This is causing all kinds of problems and the
           Russians want it fixed by tomorrow. If not, then
           they might hand you over. They don't have a good
           relationship with the United States, but there's
           many other factors in play here, and if they
           bargain you against something else…

ANDREW *starts to make something with the wrapper from the chocolate.*

Do you really have any idea what you've done?

ANDREW   Yes, you've seen the interview, I'm fully aware of what I've done, of the importance of it –

MAN   But are you aware of how unbelievably dangerous it is. Not just for you – I mean it is dangerous for you, I'll come onto that in a minute – but dangerous for the United States of America. For western civilisation. For all the things you hold up as being important. Freedom. Democracy. How can we have these things if we don't have security?

ANDREW   What? – Wait – what are you saying?

MAN   I'm making the case that from their point of view. You are a child. You may have a noble cause, as you see it, but you are thinking short-term, the next year or two, maybe the next decade, you're not thinking of the broader Churchillian sweep of history. And in that sweep, the institutions which you have cracked open, and sought to destroy, are the very foundations of the society you rely on.

ANDREW   Those institutions mean nothing if… oh god… look, I'm really sorry but I'm not going through all this again, these arguments, I'm tired and we can do this another time.

He carries on making the model…

Pause.

The MAN *watches him.*

MAN   There are people that want to cut your head off.

Beat.

There are people that want to cut my head off too.

And the only thing, in the end that's stopping them cutting all our heads off, or setting off a bomb full of nails right next to us, is the security services. Is their ability, essentially, to predict the future.

ANDREW   You can have a drink if you want.

MAN   No thank you.

And you, by doing what you've done, have torn that system open. Every American citizen, every British citizen, every two-year-old child in those countries is going to become more vulnerable to attack because you will have taken away their ability to protect their own people.

ANDREW   I thought you said you worked for him.

MAN   I do.

ANDREW   Then why are you making this argument, surely –

MAN   There are things that have to be done in the dark.

ANDREW   Is this a lesson or –

MAN   There are things –

ANDREW   A tutorial – cos I'm not as young as I look – I am aware –

MAN   That have to be done to protect society, to enable society to function that society doesn't like, doesn't want to know about, doesn't want to see, wants to just be done, while we go out for the weekend, order a new kitchen, watch Netflix and look the other way. Drone attacks by our forces that render human beings to soup, interrogation techniques we *know* are effective but that could potentially be labelled torture if you were so-minded, and also the ability to see and hear *everything*. That last one has genuinely stopped terrorist attacks.

ANDREW   There's no evidence for that.

MAN   There is. But it's classified.

ANDREW   I'm not getting into this –

MAN   My point is that what you've done is dangerous,
             but you think you can avoid the cost. What we do
             is dangerous as well. But we're aware of the cost
             and we think it's worth doing it anyway.

ANDREW   I've been very careful about how this information
             is released, it's not like how you did it, I went to
             journalists and even now they're going through it,
             carefully redacting names.

MAN   There will be a mistake.

ANDREW   No, they've reassured me –

MAN   There will be a mistake, there always is. At least
             one person will die because of what you've done.

ANDREW   I don't think that's inevitable at all.

MAN   And the terrifying thought for you to contemplate
             right now is.

             That person could be you.

             ANDREW *finishes making the model. It's an
             intricate star.*

             The American people didn't know that the United
             States was involved in torture, until it was revealed.

             Or mass surveillance, until you made it public.

             Perhaps there's other things they don't know about.

             Like assassination. Like sending someone to
             another country to take out a problem.

             And Andrew, you are one of your country's
             biggest problems at the moment.

ANDREW   They wouldn't dare kill me. That would be too
             obvious –

MAN   It would look like you took your own life.

             They would send someone in. Who was
             experienced. And who could pretend to be
             someone you wanted to be close to.

             An associate.

Then that person would, who would be an experienced professional, would arrange your death in such a way that it would look like all the attention, everything you'd done, had become too much, and so – now the work is over – you'd ended it all.

And were now dead. You now didn't exist. Those thoughts in your head, that you're thinking right now, would stop.

Reality would cease. Everything you did this for, wouldn't matter, because the world would to all intents and purposes, to you, finish.

ANDREW   What are you... are you threatening me?

MAN   I'm saying the current danger level, to you, is very high.

I'm saying I could be anyone.

I'm saying perhaps I'm not working for him. I only said that so you'd let me in.

Perhaps I'm working for someone else, and you are about to die so quickly that you'll never know the truth.

I'm saying what was in the chocolate.

Nothing. There was nothing in the chocolate but would you like to be protected against that threat for the foreseeable future?

We can do that.

I can do that.

Are you crying?

Long pause.

We would like you to agree to work with us. To help us out. And in return. We'll look after you.

ANDREW   I... uh... okay... I'm... my head is...

MAN   What?

ANDREW   I'm not feeling that well.

MAN   Why not?

ANDREW   Oh god.

MAN   Just agree.

ANDREW   No.

MAN   Agree to work with us, and we'll take care of everything.

ANDREW   Who was the woman?

MAN   As I explained, she could have been anyone. Without proper resources you can never be sure. Anyone you meet from now, might be a threat.

ANDREW   Can you come back?

MAN   What?

ANDREW   Come back in the morning.

MAN   Leave you overnight?

ANDREW   Yeah.

MAN   I can but it's normally done overnight.

                Death.

ANDREW   I just... need time.

                Please.

                The MAN *looks at him for a while.*

MAN   How about another bar of chocolate?

                He takes it out. ANDREW *looks for a moment.*

                Or not.

                ANDREW *reaches for it.*

                The MAN *moves it away.*

                When you say yes.

The MAN *looks at him for a while.*

Don't open the door to anyone.

He goes.

ANDREW *sits.*

Stares.

Alone.

3.

The night.

ANDREW *is doing sit-ups without his top on.*

A knock at the door.

ANDREW *stops for a moment.*

Then carries on with the sit-ups.

Another knock at the door.

A moment. ANDREW *carries on.*

ANDREW   It's locked.

> *The* WOMAN *comes in. She's looking possibly
> a little drunk, her hair is more relaxed than before.
> She holds a bag.*

WOMAN   Hi! Just checking if – Wow. Okay. Why have you?
Okay. Should I come back at some other time?

ANDREW   No. It's fine.

WOMAN   Why have you got your shirt off?

ANDREW   I was exercising.

WOMAN   It's very late at night.

ANDREW   I couldn't sleep.

WOMAN   You know there's a gym downstairs? It's actually
not bad, I mean the facilities here aren't great
generally you have to pay through the nose for
wifi, and the bar's okay if you can get past the
prostitutes. Who by the way all have laptops. They
sit there at tables and do what look like accounts
on Excel on their Macbook Airs when they're not
chatting to men or being fucked. I mean, I just
have so many feelings about that in so many
directions, the rights and wrongs of that because

no doubt these women are being so much better paid than I am, but would I do what they do? No I would not. Am I in a position, really to make that call? To say what I would do in their position? No I am not, because the alternatives might all be horrific. Sorry I'm rambling, I do that when it's late and I've been having fun, the point is the gym's okay. You could do exercise in the gym.

ANDREW   I'm not allowed to leave my room.

WOMAN   Oh yeah. Forgot.

ANDREW   …

WOMAN   I could send one of those prostitutes up.

ANDREW   No thanks.

WOMAN   She could dress like Mindy. Use a false name. You could use a false name too.

And only speak through writing pictures on pieces of paper.

Or better, not speak at all.

And no eye contact.

Ultimate privacy. Total silence.

ANDREW   I'm fine thanks.

WOMAN   You ever used a prostitute?

ANDREW   No.

WOMAN   Me neither. I think it must be horrible, but it's one of those things isn't it, that's sort of become so acceptable in society it's easy not to think about it, but if you imagine actually letting someone invade you like that –

ANDREW   I thought you'd have gone by now.

WOMAN   Gone? No. I'm staying here. Waiting for you to change your mind.

ANDREW   You're not who you say you are.

WOMAN   I know, I told you that. I explained the reasons why.

ANDREW   I mean you don't work for him. The other man.
Also called George. He came and said they don't
know anything about you.

WOMAN   What other man?

ANDREW   George.

Beat.

WOMAN   We don't work with anyone called George.

ANDREW   You mean…

WOMAN   Did he say he worked for us?

ANDREW   With him. He said he was sent by him to speak
to me.

WOMAN   No that's me. That's what I'm here to do. This
other man. Lying to you. Describe him.

ANDREW   He's –

WOMAN   He probably works for the Russian Government.
Or a newspaper. A Russian newspaper. Or worse.
He could even be a blogger Andrew.

Did he threaten you?

Who knows? But whoever, or *whatever* he was, *or
is*, it's got nothing to do with us.

ANDREW   But are you going to find out about him?

WOMAN   You get people like that all the time.

ANDREW   It doesn't bother you.

WOMAN   Nah.

ANDREW   I thought you were protecting me?

WOMAN   Well as I said, it's hard for me to justify that if
you're not one of us.

Pause.

You're in a bit of mess aren't you?

Long pause.

ANDREW   I think there's going to be a war.

           Beat.

WOMAN   Have you gone all –

ANDREW   I'm serious.

WOMAN   Okay. Okay, but with your shirt off, and saying
           things like that it makes me think you're either
           like Brando in *Apocalypse Now*, or that you're
           about to go on some kind of mass killing – when
           you say war –

ANDREW   Have you got a bank account?

WOMAN   So we're sort of skitting between topics here?

ANDREW   …

WOMAN   Yes, I have got a bank account. I've got several
           actually. Different banks. Different names in fact,
           but that's –

ANDREW   Do you trust that your money will be there? When
           you want it?

WOMAN   Yes.

ANDREW   …

WOMAN   No. That's why I have the money in different
           banks.

ANDREW   In different countries I expect as well.

WOMAN   Yes.

ANDREW   So you don't trust the banks.

WOMAN   Okay, there's a glimpse here of where this is
           going –

ANDREW   You don't trust the government, we've established
           that.

WOMAN   Right.

ANDREW   God?

WOMAN   Yes? Oh sorry, you weren't talking to me.

ANDREW   Do you trust God?

WOMAN   No Andrew of course I don't trust God.

ANDREW   Or the church.

WOMAN   Ha!

ANDREW   …

WOMAN   *No*.

ANDREW   We're ruling things out. Aren't we? Free-market
capitalism.

WOMAN   I'm on the left.

ANDREW   Marxism then?

WOMAN   Wouldn't it be great if it actually worked though?

ANDREW   The law.

WOMAN   Of course not.

ANDREW   Police

WOMAN   Ha ha.

ANDREW   What then? What do you, with your degrees, and
your self-proclaimed passion, what do you believe
in? The thing that you tie your spirit and your
work and your exertion to, what is the set of
values that gets you through the day?

WOMAN   Progress.

          We get better.

ANDREW   I see no evidence for that.

          Long pause.

WOMAN   Wifi!

ANDREW   What?

WOMAN   We've never had wifi before. And yes, I know
that sounds facetious and I know you're feeling
this passionately so bear with me – but we
literally in the history of civilisation, have never

invented or used wifi before, the dinosaurs didn't have it, the Victorians didn't have it, we didn't have it in the nineties.

ANDREW   That's progress?

WOMAN   That's an example. Violence across the world is down. Poverty is down. Education is up. Emancipation of women is up. We're not doing as badly as you think.

ANDREW   We're heading for something bad.

WOMAN   Maybe. But when that's done, we'll move on.

ANDREW   Yeah but actually when that's done you'll be dead and I'll be dead, I'm not talking about a small war like the Second World War, I'm talking about a complete and global collapse of every state, of every institution. We're like – that – far away. It's about to happen. We can't see it because we're hiding behind the walls but if you live in Sudan, Kenya, Iraq, Syria, Tunisia, Greece, Ukraine – you've felt literally felt on your skin the effect of this collapse. You know, in a way that we don't yet, what is about to happen.

WOMAN   No wifi.

ANDREW   No water, electricity, no food, no security, yes no wifi. This isn't a sort of conspiracy thing, this is real. And it will happen not because it needs to but because we don't trust anyone. We've all lost faith. As the rich get richer, and the politicians become so detached they cannot speak without hypocrisy, as the average experience means increasingly nothing, and resentment grows, when we all believe in nothing and credit, trust, is gone, it will all crumble.

Beat.

In many ways it already has.

WOMAN   You're going through a thing tonight, aren't you? It makes sense.

ANDREW   That's why I did it. Released all that stuff.
           Because the only way to stabilise our faith in what
           we're doing is to see the contradictions – expose
           the systems – and discuss and then move towards
           something we can get behind. Something more
           fair, more open and transparent. Not authority but
           real consent.

WOMAN   Yeah. That's right. Exactly. That's what we
           think too.

ANDREW   I don't know what you think. You don't articulate
           it. You're more into secrets than any of them.

WOMAN   To protect ourselves.

ANDREW   Well that's not going to work, so here's my deal,
           George. You tell me who you really are, your real
           name, and then I'll get on board. You trust me. I'll
           trust you. And we'll save the world.

WOMAN   Alright. Well. My real name is Sarah.

           Sarah Lishman.

           Pause.

           Sorry. That's not true.

           This is hard. Alright. Actually? Really...?

           I'm Charlotte. Waters.

           Pause.

           Or am I?

           You see this is impossible. I could just be making
           stuff up. How do I prove it? You know what I
           mean? Apart from saying that I'm this lady stood
           in this room with this face and body how do I go
           about proving to you in a way that will be
           acceptable, who I really am?

           He doesn't answer.

           *She reaches into the bag, and gives him a plastic
           cowboy hat.*

I got this from one of the girls downstairs. It was
one of her props, and I thought since you were
American, then you'd like it.

ANDREW   …

WOMAN   An outlaw.

ANDREW   …

WOMAN   Howdee.

Pause.

ANDREW   It was what they wanted. Not just the founding
fathers but the pilgrim fathers. When they got on
the boat. They sought a place they could start
again and act how they wanted. Free from
authority and the systems that held them. They
wanted to make something new and they did.

WOMAN   After they wiped out the people who were already
there. And before the country fell into an
essentially lawless state for quite a few decades.

ANDREW   Yeah.

Pause.

I've never felt less free. Whether I'm in this room
or not. Even before I did it. I felt utterly trapped.
Between giving my bank statements for the whole
year so I could get a mortgage, and my health
payments, and my movements known to
companies, and what I like, and who I am, and
recorded on CCTV every day. Being in this room.
At least there aren't any cameras here.

WOMAN   Well…

ANDREW   Really?

WOMAN   Yeah. Probably the Russians put a couple in, that's
why they put you here. And we've got one going
too. So yeah – it's all monitored.

ANDREW   Okay.

WOMAN   Yee-ha. They'll love the hat.

          Beat.

ANDREW   Well it's going to have to be something to do with
          your body isn't it?

WOMAN   Are you aware that sounds really creepy?

ANDREW   I mean how do I know that you mean what you
          say, how do I know I'm not just one of many
          people you are lying to, and that this is
          fundamental to your life's work, well you're going
          to have to do something to yourself that's unique.
          That you haven't done before or since.

WOMAN   I'm not going to sleep with you.

ANDREW   I don't want you to sleep with me.

WOMAN   I can get one of those girls if this is just a way to
          get a bit.

ANDREW   Can you please take this seriously.

WOMAN   What then?

ANDREW   I don't know. Sacrifice something. Take your
          clothes off.

WOMAN   I'm sorry?!

ANDREW   No I don't mean – just all you've got is you, like
          you said a woman standing in a room. And we
          need to establish some trust. There's nothing else
          I can do. You know everything about me. You've
          got the resources and I've never hidden anything,
          but you need to give me something in return and
          you're absolutely right, all you've got is what's
          tangibly in this room. So I've got that far.

          You come up with something then.

          She thinks.

          Sits opposite him.

          Then takes out a safety pin from her bag.
          A relatively large one.

WOMAN   Okay. So here's my idea.

She unbends the safety pin so it's a needle. Then gets a lighter and lights the end. Holds the tip of the needle in the flame.

So that you trust me. I'm going to put this needle through my skin. This piece of skin here, between my thumb and forefinger. I will put an actual hole in it. And yes, that hole will heal, but it will leave a scar. And I don't have any other scars on my body. Not one. You can check if you like – well the bits you can see I'm not taking any clothes off – and I certainly don't have any other marks on my hands like this. So if I do this you will know that you are unique and this is real and it matters to me and that I mean what I say. What do you think?

ANDREW   Are you heating it up?

WOMAN   I think it sterilises it or something I've never really done this before and I don't have a crack habit so I'm basically a novice but it can't do any harm right.

ANDREW   Okay.

Beat.

WOMAN   You're sure you need this?

ANDREW   Yes. It's a start.

WOMAN   A 'start'! Jesus. Ready?

ANDREW   Yes.

She's about to do it.

Why does the phone have nothing in it?

She stops.

WOMAN   I'm sorry?

ANDREW   The phone. I opened it and there's nothing inside. Just a speaker and some electronics.

WOMAN   Well that's what you'd find inside a phone that's
            basically –

ANDREW   No you'd normally find something to operate the
            buttons, a little circuit board but in there it's
            literally just a speaker really.

WOMAN   You want to – shall we do this in a minute?

ANDREW   I thought it might... I thought it might be relevant.

WOMAN   Well it's the Russians they've given you a fake
            phone haven't they? Bloody Russians.

ANDREW   But it was you who said you had it disconnected.

WOMAN   I know! And now it turns out it wasn't a real
            phone anyway, waste of bloody time! Look we're
            good, Andrew, but we can't get everything right.

            ANDREW *just looks at her.*

            May I?

ANDREW   Okay.

            Beat.

WOMAN   This is really going to hurt, isn't it?

ANDREW   I would imagine.

WOMAN   You're going to let me do this?

ANDREW   I think it will help. Yes.

WOMAN   God. I'm glad I'm quite drunk. Actually get me
            that bottle of whiskey from the thing. The one
            I had before.

            He does.

            *She takes it. Drinks it. Sploshes some over the
            needle.*

            Alcohol's supposed to – oh fuck it.

            *She puts the needle through the piece of skin.
            Winces.*

ANDREW   Are you okay?

WOMAN   Yeah.

Blood comes out.

It's really painful.

She finishes.

Can you get me some tissue?

He does.

He gives it to her.

Jesus that hurt.

She stops the bleeding.

Okay. Okay.

She drinks from the whiskey.

Okay. So. Right. So. Happy?

He nods.

Good. Cos you can believe what you like but you saw that – that was like some blood, an actual bodily act. You want to see?

ANDREW   Yes.

She shows him.

WOMAN   Okay?

ANDREW   Yeah.

WOMAN   Right.

Beat.

So you see it does matter to me. To us. You matter a *huge* amount. You are unique. We do need you. I am who I say I am, and I'll always have a scar to prove it. If I did this all the time, my hand would be covered in scars, which as you can see, it's not.

So?

Are you in?

So you're in? Tomorrow we'll call him, and say
that you're on board and you'll do what we say,
and you'll let us help you.

So?

Very long pause.

ANDREW   Okay.

WOMAN   Good to have you with us.

She puts her hand out for him to shake.

You want to shake?

He doesn't. She puts her hand away.

She stands. Drinks from the whiskey.

I'll see you in the morning.

ANDREW   Yes.

WOMAN   You going to put some clothes on now?

ANDREW   Maybe.

WOMAN   You like the hat?

ANDREW   Yes.

WOMAN   Good.

Beat.

ANDREW   What are you going to do now?

WOMAN   Well I'm – surprisingly enough I'm not so tired
any more so I think I'm going to go downstairs
and get another drink and maybe a sandwich, they
do these all-night sandwiches that are only one
type – it's like ham and something but they're
very moreish so I'm going to have one or two of
those and sit and drink, and maybe you know what
even have a cigarette to mask this fucking pain
you made me go through, and I'll hang out with
the prozzies until they get carted away. And
eventually I'll fall asleep in my room and in the
morning I'll come and get you. Nine o'clock.

ANDREW   What then? In the morning.

WOMAN   Firstly, get you out of this fucking room.

ANDREW   Right.

WOMAN   Then get your position in Russia secure.

ANDREW   Okay.

WOMAN   Passport. Get you granted asylum. Get Putin
           onside. We've got calls we can make. We'll try to
           get you on the phone with him as well.

           Beat.

ANDREW   I can't believe you actually just did that.

WOMAN   Like you said. We've got to start somewhere. In
           the cold war we'd have had to sleep together to
           prove mutual trust.

           Now it's just self-mutilation.

ANDREW   Progress.

WOMAN   Exactly.

           She goes.

           He sits.

           He stands.

           He goes to the wall.

           Puts his hand on it.

4.

The next morning.

The WOMAN *and the* MAN *stand in the room with* ANDREW.

ANDREW I've been thinking about the phone.

WOMAN You know we're both here right?

ANDREW Yes, but that's not what bothers me.

WOMAN Okay.

MAN What about the phone?

ANDREW That there's nothing in it.

WOMAN He was going on about this last night –

ANDREW It doesn't make sense.

WOMAN There *is* something in it, you said there's a speaker and we told you it was the Russians.

ANDREW Yes.

WOMAN But more importantly, look! Me and George, the other one, we're both here together, are you not going to comment on that, since before we were apparently unaware of each other's existence?

ANDREW Okay. What? You met in the bar downstairs.

WOMAN No. We knew about each other, all along. We just wanted to test you. Good cop bad cop.

ANDREW Who's who?

WOMAN Isn't it obvious?

ANDREW …

WOMAN/MAN I'm *bad cop.*

WOMAN Wait –

MAN   Oh... I thought... sorry.

             (*To* ANDREW.) Slight... error.

ANDREW   It doesn't matter.

MAN   (*To* WOMAN.) I honestly thought you said –

WOMAN   Andrew this is so much not how I expected this
             would go. You don't even seem to be paying
             attention. Look, we can tell you all this now that
             you've agreed to join us, we can reveal that actually
             both him and me were working for the same side.

ANDREW   I had some of the whiskey and it wasn't really
             whiskey. It was sort of like whiskey but it was
             cheap.

WOMAN   Russia doesn't really do whiskey.

MAN   You should taste the vodka. Jesus Andrew if you
             were worrying about spending your life in Russia,
             about spending the rest of your days in a
             completely foreign country complete with actual
             Russians (and in parenthesis I *would* be worried
             about that) then the vodka is definitely some
             compensation.

ANDREW   I tried the vodka.

MAN   And?

ANDREW   It was fine.

MAN   Fine. Well maybe you don't know enough about
             vodka. The vodka is really fucking *good* –

ANDREW   What's going to happen this morning?

MAN   Possibly nothing, possibly a lot, calls have been
             made to see about that asylum that we're after,
             we've already got our best contacts speaking to
             the Russian authorities – they know they need to
             resolve this and really they want to take you in –
             I mean that's good news – they're just looking for
             a way they can take you without it seeming too
             petulant. We're going to help them with that.

WOMAN   And when we do find a way forward when we can get you out of this limbo and get you some kind of passport, we'll do a press conference but we think for the time being it's actually best if you keep your head down.

ANDREW   Right.

MAN   Until we're all on a more stable footing.

ANDREW   Will I get to speak to him? You said –

MAN   Andrew he's stuck in an embassy, in not an entirely different situation to you actually, communication is a constant challenge, especially secure communication – I assume you have some idea why – but yeah we can try to get him on the phone for you. If you'd like?

ANDREW   When?

MAN   Now.

Or later.

Probably later.

ANDREW   Can I see your hand?

WOMAN   What?

ANDREW   Can I see your hand, from last night? How it's healing.

The WOMAN *looks at the* MAN.

WOMAN   (*To* MAN.) Actually shall we try to get him on the phone now?

MAN   Now?!

WOMAN   Yes.

ANDREW   Your hand.

MAN   We can't get him now. You know that. He's probably asleep.

WOMAN   (*With an implication…*) Well shall we *try anyway*?

MAN   What?

             Sorry. Am I... Am I missing something?

ANDREW   Just show me.

             Pause. The WOMAN *rolls her eyes.*

WOMAN   Well you know what Andrew, it's actually healed
             extremely well.

ANDREW   What's happened to it?

WOMAN   Nothing. Look. Good as new.

ANDREW   But... I saw you...

WOMAN   Yeah. About that.

             She takes a fake-skin glove out of her bag.

MAN   Oh. Sorry. I get what you...

WOMAN   Old trick. Just in case. The skin wasn't real.
             Neither was the blood.

ANDREW   But... our trust. It doesn't mean anything, the fact
             that was real, that it would last, that was the whole
             point –

WOMAN   But we've made the calls now. We've told people.

ANDREW   You just happened to have a spare glove waiting?
             A sort of special prop just for the occasion.

WOMAN   If you remember, it was me that suggested it.
             Oldest trick in the book. Well not oldest, but you
             know, old.

             Still got the hat?

             Pause.

ANDREW   I knocked on the wall. It doesn't sound like a wall.

WOMAN   Where are you going with this? Are you going a
             bit mad Andrew, should we be calling a
             psychiatrist or something?

ANDREW   Do it. Yourself.

             Knock on the wall.

MAN	No I'm not going to knock on the –
	The WOMAN *knocks on the wall.*
WOMAN	Oh yeah.
	He's right. It doesn't sound like a wall.
	She does it again.
	It's kind of more hollow, and more soft, at the same time.
	Long pause.
	ANDREW *tests the floor. Listens to it.*
MAN	Should we…?
WOMAN	Maybe.
	Beat.
MAN	Sorry can I just ask while we've got a moment, am I good or bad cop then?
WOMAN	Bad.
MAN	*Right.* Okay then. Bad… okay…
WOMAN	Andrew there is a reason the wall is how you described.
ANDREW	I thought so.
	I'm not in a hotel, am I?
	Beat.
MAN	No.
ANDREW	None of this is a real hotel.
WOMAN	No.
ANDREW	Didn't think so.
	ANDREW *picks up the chair and throws it at the wall.*
	It disappears through a previously unseen gap. Which has been there the whole time. An optical illusion.

The MAN *lights a cigarette.*

MAN   He's not stupid.

WOMAN   Well we know that. We do know that but I thought
           he might last a little bit longer.

ANDREW   You don't work for him.

           Do you?

           Either of you.

           Pause.

WOMAN   No.

ANDREW   Who do you work for?

WOMAN   Well that's a really difficult question because the
           thing is that these days –

           She presses a button and one wall switches off.

           – these different groups whether they're
           government agencies or companies or terrorist
           organisations well they're all rather connected
           aren't they?

           *She takes one corner of one of the walls and peels
           it away.*

           Bearing in mind the way that governments need
           companies and companies need influence and
           influence comes through paying people of the
           kind that you might in an ideal world not want to
           be paying, and even if you can draw lines
           between all these different groups those lines
           don't hold do they?

           She presses another button and the ceiling lifts up.

           And the ideologies behind them are so indistinct
           and ever-changing, in fact I would go as far as to
           say that the only constant we can refer to is power.

           *She starts folding up some of the various hotel
           props and furniture. Some of them she deflates.*

I would say I work for power, and I want that
power for my own self-preservation and to get
the things I want. Oh. Well that's a much clearer
answer than I was expecting to give. There you
go Andrew.

ANDREW   I thought you might be Russian?

WOMAN   Do I sound Russian?   ·

ANDREW   It wouldn't make any difference if you did.

MAN   I'm not Russian either.

ANDREW   I want to speak to the ambassador.

MAN   The ambassador has washed his hands of you
Andrew we discussed that right at the very
beginning – with the exception of a few journalists
who have zero clout, you have no one. Everyone
is backing away from you as fast as they can –
well anyone who can help you. They're pleased,
some of them, that you did what you did, but that
is done and now you're old news.

ANDREW   In that case.

WOMAN   What did you want?

ANDREW   What?

WOMAN   What did you hope for, when you pressed the
button and all that information trickled or flooded
out of the Pentagon what did you hope would be
the result?

ANDREW   That people would know the truth.

WOMAN   What truth? What people? The truth that they
were being spied on. They don't care. They like
it. It makes them feel safer. If it keeps the war
out there and not in their homes they don't mind.
They wilfully would rather not think about it.
You mean people like you. Thinkers. Theorists.
Warriors for the good and proper. There aren't
very many of you.

ANDREW   Courage is contagious.

The WOMAN *smiles, patronisingly.*

WOMAN   Aw.

Not really.

Not when there's free wifi and Netflix.

We're left in a large empty space.

ANDREW   There are people who want progress. Like you said –

WOMAN   But the documents you leaked all the files I mean fine it revealed that the government was lying on a massive scale to the people and it made us think that possibly everyone is lying all the time. But that's not the revelation is it? That's not the unexpected thing.

The unexpected aspect in all of this, and Facebook are surprised, the government is surprised, in fact everyone in power is surprised, is how much of this the people are prepared to take. All the information of where you go and who you are and what you do and who you love and what you eat and what you look like what you think what your body does or doesn't do, your experiences and photos and history and dreams are all given away in an instant as long as the product is supposedly free. Well no one saw that coming. The shoppers will take off their clothes and shred every last piece of their dignity if it means they can get something free. Who knew?

And in that context you releasing these files, is it any wonder the response is going to be a big shrug?

You think you're revealing how you can't trust anyone? We know. But we do it anyway. Why? It's easier.

MAN   Suddenly you don't *own* your music, you have to hire it. Has anyone complained?

WOMAN   That's *actually* the thing that bothers him most. Spotify. He's really shallow. You can't trust anyone Andrew that's absolutely right. And you can't trust anything. Any system of ownership or rights is totally contingent on forces that nobody understands, not really, so the whole world is just… tilting at the moment. Just rocking on the edge… And what you did?

ANDREW   I tipped it over.

WOMAN   No. You merely pointed at it.

Pause.

We've been having fun and games with you.

ANDREW   Why?

MAN   So you're just like everyone else.

ANDREW   What do you –

WOMAN   To get you to the point where you don't know which way's up.

The whole room suddenly tilts ninety degrees.

ANDREW'*s gravity stays on his floor.*

The MAN *and the* WOMAN *walk round so their floor is the old wall.*

ANDREW   How are you doing this?

WOMAN   You want to know the mechanics?

MAN   He actually does.

WOMAN   It's all about perception. You want more detail?

I can tell you exactly if you like but it's really not the point.

ANDREW *sits down.*

Long pause.

ANDREW   Can I leave?

WOMAN   Andrew, I'm not sure you get this. Your passport
          has been revoked. You have no papers whatsoever.

          Until you *join* something, sign up to *something*,
          it's not a question of can you leave, it's a question
          of that you don't exist.

          Pause.

MAN   Do you want us to try and get you a Russian
          passport?

ANDREW   The Russians are more corrupt than us, if I was to
          become a Russian citizen that would be –

MAN   But you'll be able to stay here, under our
          protection.

ANDEW   Under your control.

MAN   Yes.

ANDREW   But I don't know who you are.

WOMAN   Anonymity is a luxury granted to those in power.

          You don't know who anybody truly important is.
          And they will keep it like that.

MAN   Look do you want a passport or not? We've got
          a deal?

          Long pause.

ANDREW   Okay. A Russian passport. Fine.

MAN   *Alright.* Good. *No* thanks is there? No gratitude.
          You should come down from there by the way.
          The floor's over here.

          He goes.

          Another long pause.

          Everything's spinning.

WOMAN   You must feel better.

          Now you've joined something.

          Pause.

You know you were talking about war?

I've seen war.

And if I had to describe what it was like?

If I had to say what it actually feels like. Leaving aside the pain and the blood and the kind of *aesthetic* of it – I mean if I tried to describe what it does to your mind and your experience...

She gets a safety pin out. Undoes it.

It's like this.

It feels exactly like what you're feeling now.

Utterly wild.

She holds the needle out, then presses it against herself and this time...

...she pops, like a balloon.

ANDREW *is left on stage alone.*

Staring.

For slightly longer than we expect.

Then blackout.

End.